FEARLESS
CONVERSATION™

WHY IS GRACE SO AMAZING?

DISCUSSIONS FROM ACTS, ROMANS, 1-2 CORINTHIANS, GALATIANS, EPHESIANS, AND 1 THESSALONIANS

PARTICIPANT GUIDE

Loveland, CO

Group
Real. Bold. Love.

Group resources really work!

This Group resource incorporates our R.E.A.L. approach to ministry. It reinforces a growing friendship with Jesus, encourages long-term learning, and results in life transformation, because it's:

Relational—Learner-to-learner interaction enhances learning and builds Christian friendships.

Experiential—What learners experience through discussion and action sticks with them up to 9 times longer than what they simply hear or read.

Applicable—The aim of Christian education is to equip learners to be both hearers and doers of God's Word.

Learner-based—Learners understand and retain more when the learning process takes into consideration how they learn best.

Fearless Conversation: Why Is Grace So Amazing?

Discussions from Acts, Romans, 1-2 Corinthians, Galatians, Ephesians, and 1 Thessalonians

Participant Guide

Copyright © 2014 Group Publishing, Inc.

Visit our website: group.com

Fearless Conversation adult Sunday school curriculum is created by the amazing adult ministry team at Group. Contributing writers for this quarter are:

Jill Wuellner • Susan Lawrence • Larry Shallenberger • Amy Simpson

Unless otherwise indicated, all Scripture quotations are taken from the *Holy Bible*, New International Version® NIV® Copyright © 1973, 1978, 1984, 2011 by Biblica, Inc.® Used by permission. All rights reserved worldwide.

ISBN 978-1-4707-1682-0

Printed in the United States of America

10 9 8 7 6 5 4 3 2 1   21 20 19 18 17 16 15 14

CONTENTS

HERE'S WHAT A LESSON LOOKS LIKE

Your leader will guide each lesson through four sections:

GREETING

Make new friends and start the conversation as the topic of the week is introduced.

GROUNDING

This is where you read the Scripture for the week. The Bible content is always provided here in the participant guide. After hearing God's Word read aloud, you'll have the opportunity to follow the inductive study method of writing down first responses, questions, thoughts, or ideas that are sparked by the Bible reading.

GRAPPLING

Here's where the conversation deepens. You'll find questions that are intentionally challenging to answer. These won't have easy answers and you won't have a fill-in-the-blank option. Everyone will wrestle with the questions that the lesson provides, as well as their own questions that they're wondering about. The leader will ask God to guide the conversation—and you can join in that prayer! Remember to treat others with respect during these conversations, even if you don't agree with them. Listen first. Speak second.

GROWING

Here's where the personal application comes in. You'll have the chance to reflect on what God's Word, as shared in this lesson, means to you for your own life and determine what your personal response is.

Throughout each lesson you'll also find two other helps:

BEHIND THE SCENES

These sections of commentary and notes from Bible scholars will give you additional context into history, language, culture, and other relevant information. You can read these sections ahead of time or during the lesson—whichever works best for you.

GOING DEEPER

These tips will help you be a great conversationalist. They remind you how to keep a conversation going, how to be a better listener, and how to be respectful even if you don't agree with someone.

FINAL TIP:

Have a sense of divine anticipation. Approach each class with a heart full of anticipation over what God might do that day. God is alive and present with you and your class. Always prepare by praying, asking God to help you see his hand at work in the conversation. Trust God to show up and show you and others in the class exactly where he wants the conversation to go!

LESSON 1: CAN GOD CHANGE SOMEONE— EVEN IF THEY DON'T WANT TO BE CHANGED?

GREETING

What are the little pet peeves that drive you crazy?

When someone else asks you to change, what's your initial reaction? Be honest!

GROUNDING

God's Word: Acts 9:1-19

[1] Meanwhile, Saul was still breathing out murderous threats against the Lord's disciples. He went to the high priest [2] and asked him for letters to the synagogues in Damascus, so that if he found any there who belonged to the Way, whether men or women, he might take them as prisoners to Jerusalem. [3] As he neared Damascus on his journey, suddenly a light from heaven flashed around him. [4] He fell to the ground and heard a voice say to him, "Saul, Saul, why do you persecute me?"

[5] "Who are you, Lord?" Saul asked.

"I am Jesus, whom you are persecuting," he replied. [6] "Now get up and go into the city, and you will be told what you must do."

[7] The men traveling with Saul stood there speechless; they heard the sound but did not see anyone. [8] Saul got up from the ground, but when he opened his eyes he could see nothing. So they led him by the hand into Damascus. [9] For three days he was blind, and did not eat or drink anything.

[10] In Damascus there was a disciple named Ananias. The Lord called to him in a vision, "Ananias!"

"Yes, Lord," he answered.

[11] The Lord told him, "Go to the house of Judas on Straight Street and ask for a man from Tarsus named Saul, for he is praying. [12] In a vision he has seen a man named Ananias come and place his hands on him to restore his sight."

▶

[13] "Lord," Ananias answered, "I have heard many reports about this man and all the harm he has done to your holy people in Jerusalem. [14] And he has come here with authority from the chief priests to arrest all who call on your name."

[15] But the Lord said to Ananias, "Go! This man is my chosen instrument to proclaim my name to the Gentiles and their kings and to the people of Israel. [16] I will show him how much he must suffer for my name."

[17] Then Ananias went to the house and entered it. Placing his hands on Saul, he said, "Brother Saul, the Lord—Jesus, who appeared to you on the road as you were coming here—has sent me so that you may see again and be filled with the Holy Spirit." [18] Immediately, something like scales fell from Saul's eyes, and he could see again. He got up and was baptized, [19] and after taking some food, he regained his strength.

Saul spent several days with the disciples in Damascus.

What are the first questions that come to mind? What catches your attention?

Capture those thoughts here.

GRAPPLING

GOING DEEPER

You can help others in your group go deeper by listening with your full attention and by asking questions as others share. Saying "I wonder about what you just said. Tell me more!" will help people know you care about what they're saying and want them to open up more.

BEHIND THE SCENES

Saul wasn't your typical guy. In Philippians 3:4-6 he gives us a glimpse of some of his achievements and reasons for confidence in himself. His Jewish pedigree was impeccable. He was born of the tribe of Benjamin, meaning he could trace his lineage back hundreds of years to Benjamin, the brother of Joseph. He was a Pharisee, one of the Jewish elite, and kept to the letter of the Mosaic law. Paul says he kept the law so well that he was considered "faultless." His passion for protecting the Jewish teachings and law was so great he was willing to persecute others who taught something he viewed as heresy.

You'll find "Behind the Scenes" boxes with Bible commentary provided throughout this lesson. You can read these ahead of time or as you move through the lesson. They're there to help you gain a better understanding of the Bible.

Why do you think Jesus used such dramatic means for changing Saul?

Verses 15 and 16 of this chapter say, "But the Lord said to Ananias, 'Go! This man is my chosen instrument to proclaim my name to the Gentiles and their kings and to the people of Israel. I will show him how much he must suffer for my name.'" What do you think is meant by this statement?

INTERESTING THOUGHTS SPARKED BY OTHERS IN MY GROUP:

BEHIND THE SCENES

Just before the events in today's passage from Acts 9, Stephen, known as the first Christian martyr, had been stoned by members of the Sanhedrin, which was the highest judicial council in the Jewish community. The stoning, which led to the persecution of other Christians and caused disciples to scatter to other cities, had been witnessed and approved by Saul (Acts 8:1). The disciples fleeing to other parts of Israel wasn't such a bad thing, as it allowed them to tell others about Jesus who otherwise might not have heard about him. But this dispersion from Jerusalem wasn't enough for Saul, as he "was still breathing out murderous threats against the Lord's disciples" (Acts 9:1). Saul was so determined, he was willing to make a six-day journey of approximately 140 miles on foot to Damascus to root out followers of Jesus.

PARTICIPANT GUIDE

BEHIND THE SCENES

You've heard the terms "disciple" and "apostle," but what do they mean? Are they the same? Interestingly, they aren't. An apostle is literally "a messenger or envoy." In the Bible, these are the 12 men who followed Jesus. They saw him, talked with him, and were sent by Jesus to "make disciples of all nations" (Matthew 28:19). Paul (Saul) is also included as an apostle, as Jesus spoke to him specifically and called him to be a messenger to the Gentiles.

But when reading the Bible, we tend to think of the 12 men who followed Jesus as "the 12 disciples." Disciple is a term for the follower of a specific teacher. Generally, a disciple isn't a casual follower, as one might listen occasionally to a preacher they hear on the radio. Rather, a disciple adheres to the teachings of the master and imitates him. Ananias was a disciple of Jesus who trusted so much in him that he was willing to risk his life when Jesus asked him to help Saul. How does his devotion and obedience challenge you?

Which do you think shows the power of Jesus more—an experience like Saul's, or a transformation that might take years? Explain your reasoning.

BEHIND THE SCENES

Have you ever heard the saying, "Nothing is wasted in God's economy?" Meaning, nothing in your life is wasted. God will use every experience in some way, either to change you or to change others. This was true in Saul's life. Although he was a Jew, he had been raised in Tarsus, so he was familiar with Greek culture. As a Pharisee, he also knew the Jewish tradition, theology, and Law quite well. Additionally, he was a Roman citizen, which brought a host of benefits he would need while traveling and telling others about Jesus. God used his passion, training, and upbringing in ways Paul never expected. Imagine what God can do with you!

GROWING

BEHIND THE SCENES

It's interesting to note that prior to his transformation by Jesus, Saul was bent on persecuting those who followed Jesus. Yet after his transformation as he traveled to tell others about Jesus, he was arrested, jailed, and ultimately killed for his own faith in Christ.

Take a few minutes right now to have a fearless conversation with Jesus about what's on your heart after reading this section of the Bible.

Write your personal response here.

PARTICIPANT GUIDE

LESSON 2: WHY SHOULD I PRAISE GOD WHEN MY LIFE IS HARD?

GREETING

When did you go through a hard situation but learned something in the process?

What are you going through right now, or have gone through recently, that you would describe as "hard"?

◗GROUNDING

God's Word: Acts 16:16-34

[16] Once when we were going to the place of prayer, we were met by a female slave who had a spirit by which she predicted the future. She earned a great deal of money for her owners by fortune-telling. [17] She followed Paul and the rest of us, shouting, "These men are servants of the Most High God, who are telling you the way to be saved." [18] She kept this up for many days. Finally Paul became so annoyed that he turned around and said to the spirit, "In the name of Jesus Christ I command you to come out of her!" At that moment the spirit left her.

[19] When her owners realized that their hope of making money was gone, they seized Paul and Silas and dragged them into the marketplace to face the authorities. [20] They brought them before the magistrates and said, "These men are Jews, and are throwing our city into an uproar [21] by advocating customs unlawful for us Romans to accept or practice."

[22] The crowd joined in the attack against Paul and Silas, and the magistrates ordered them to be stripped and beaten with rods. [23] After they had been severely flogged, they were thrown into prison, and the jailer was commanded to guard them carefully. [24] When he received these orders, he put them in the inner cell and fastened their feet in the stocks.

[25] About midnight Paul and Silas were praying and singing hymns to God, and the other prisoners were listening to them. [26] Suddenly there was such a violent earthquake that the foundations of the prison were shaken. At once all the prison doors flew open, and everyone's chains came loose. [27] The jailer woke up, and when he saw the prison doors open, he drew his sword and was about to kill himself because he thought the prisoners had escaped. [28] But Paul shouted, "Don't harm yourself! We are all here!"

PARTICIPANT GUIDE

²⁹ The jailer called for lights, rushed in and fell trembling before Paul and Silas. ³⁰ He then brought them out and asked, "Sirs, what must I do to be saved?"

³¹ They replied, "Believe in the Lord Jesus, and you will be saved—you and your household." ³² Then they spoke the word of the Lord to him and to all the others in his house. ³³ At that hour of the night the jailer took them and washed their wounds; then immediately he and all his household were baptized. ³⁴ The jailer brought them into his house and set a meal before them; he was filled with joy because he had come to believe in God—he and his whole household.

What questions immediately come to mind? What catches your attention?

Jot your initial thoughts and questions here.

BEHIND THE SCENES

The young fortune-teller followed Paul and Silas for several days, shouting, "These men are servants of the Most High God, who are telling you the way to be saved" (Acts 16:17-18). Paul became so annoyed he confronted the evil spirit in her. At first glance, it seems what she was saying might have helped them, but Paul would have known God's spirit and presence versus a fraud. The slave girl could have possibly created a distraction to Paul's teaching, rather than helping gather attention for the right reasons. Note that Paul did not confront the girl but the spirit. He was not irritated with the girl but with the evil spirit in her. What does this teach you about how to recognize counterfeit faith and confront it?

GRAPPLING

GOING DEEPER

We're all different. Some of us like to speak up, and some of us are more reserved. Some people are more familiar with the Bible than others. Some need lots of processing time, and others quickly connect the dots or reach a conclusion. We have different experiences and questions. And we can learn from one another! Take a deep breath and take it all in. Learn from others, and let others learn from you by asking questions and sharing with respect for others.

BEHIND THE SCENES

Paul and Silas were arrested for interfering with the income the young fortune-teller's owners could make. Once Paul commanded the evil spirit to leave her, she could no longer make her owners a profit. The owners accused Paul and Silas of stirring up civil disorder by promoting customs that were not legal for Romans. Paul and Silas had the right to share their own beliefs. Romans tolerated variant religions, but their law prohibited anything that spurred civil disorder, whether it was based in religion or otherwise.

Consider what happens in verses 16-24. Compare how hard the situation was for Paul and Silas at this time to how difficult situations can be in your own life. What can you relate to in their situation, and what seems very different from your own circumstances?

We know what happened after Paul and Silas prayed and sang—but when they were in that moment, they didn't know what was ahead. What could prompt anyone—Paul and Silas or us—to pray and sing when life is very hard?

From this account, what can we learn about the impact that our responses during hard times can have on others?

INTERESTING THOUGHTS SPARKED BY OTHERS IN MY GROUP:

BEHIND THE SCENES

When the jailer woke up and realized the doors were open, he nearly killed himself, but Paul let him know all the prisoners were still there. Jailers were personally responsible for the security of the prisoners. If a prisoner escaped, the jailer on duty would have to serve the remainder of that prisoner's sentence. In this case, he would have had to serve the sentences of all the prisoners.

Paul's response to the jailer shows his compassion. His focus wasn't on escape from the prison. He was concerned with escape of another kind—escape *toward* something instead of *from* something. He praised God despite his own circumstances and honored God by caring for the jailer's life. In turn, the jailer showed compassion to the prisoners by taking them home and tending to their wounds, and he chose to believe in the God whose power he personally witnessed for his own, as well as his family's, salvation.

GROWING

How are you struggling with praising God even when your life is hard? Or how are you struggling to praise God regardless of what's going on around you? Do you wonder what praise really is and if God is worth it?

Write your reflections here.

LESSON 3: CAN I BE GOOD ENOUGH TO PLEASE GOD?

GREETING

Is it important to do everything well? Is it really necessary to do anything perfectly?

A world-renown and celebrity chef is coming for a barbecue, and your group needs to prepare the meal he will be eating. As a group, decide what you'll prepare for this grill master and culinary expert. What will you make that will impress and amaze him with the incredible food you can create?

How do you think this activity of trying to impress a famous, professional chef relates to us trying to impress God?

GROUNDING

God's Word: Galatians 3:1-14

[1] You foolish Galatians! Who has bewitched you? Before your very eyes Jesus Christ was clearly portrayed as crucified. [2] I would like to learn just one thing from you: Did you receive the Spirit by the works of the law, or by believing what you heard? [3] Are you so foolish? After beginning by means of the Spirit, are you now trying to finish by means of the flesh? [4] Have you experienced so much in vain—if it really was in vain? [5] So again I ask, does God give you his Spirit and work miracles among you by the works of the law, or by your believing what you heard? [6] So also Abraham "believed God, and it was credited to him as righteousness."

[7] Understand, then, that those who have faith are children of Abraham. [8] Scripture foresaw that God would justify the Gentiles by faith, and announced the gospel in advance to Abraham: "All nations will be blessed through you." [9] So those who rely on faith are blessed along with Abraham, the man of faith.

[10] For all who rely on the works of the law are under a curse, as it is written: "Cursed is everyone who does not continue to do everything written in the Book of the Law." [11] Clearly no one who relies on the law is justified before God, because "the righteous will live by faith." [12] The law is not based on faith; on the contrary, it says, "The person who does these things will live by them." [13] Christ redeemed us from the curse of the law by becoming a curse for us, for it is written: "Cursed is everyone who is hung on a pole." [14] He redeemed us in order that the blessing given to Abraham might come to the Gentiles through Christ Jesus, so that by faith we might receive the promise of the Spirit.

PARTICIPANT GUIDE

What questions come to mind as you read Paul's words to the Christians in Galatia? What catches your attention?

Capture those initial thoughts here.

GRAPPLING

GOING DEEPER

You can help others in your group go deeper by listening with your full attention and by asking questions as others share. Saying "I wonder about what you just said. Tell me more!" will help people know you care about what they're saying and want them to open up more.

BEHIND THE SCENES

Unlike the letters Paul wrote to the Philippians, Ephesians, Colossians, and Thessalonians, the letter to the Galatians wasn't written to one church in a specific city. Rather, Galatia was a region in what is today central Turkey. It's unclear where the churches were located in the region, as Galatians could refer to an ethnic people or have a political meaning.

Sometime in the third century, Celtic tribes (also known as Gauls) came to this region to serve as warriors and mercenaries in what is now northern Turkey, but they ultimately overtook and settled the northern portion of Galatia. By New Testament times, the Greeks had settled in the southern portion of Galatia and were politically "Galatian" but not ethnically so, as the Celtic tribes were. Bible scholars have attempted to determine where the churches Paul ministered to were located, but since no one knows specifically when the letter was written, it's a mystery impossible to solve.

How do Christians try to "work" for acceptance before God? In light of this passage, how do you think God views that attempt for acceptance?

BEHIND THE SCENES

Understandably, Paul felt responsible for the churches he planted and to those people he converted to Christianity. He often wrote letters of encouragement and correction to those he met on his evangelistic journeys. This letter to the churches of Galatia was written because Paul had heard that Judaizers had been spreading false teaching. What is a Judaizer, you ask? This term refers to someone who influences others to adopt Jewish practices. In this instance, it was most likely Jewish Christians who were urging the Galatian Christians to add works to their faith. They believed that if they kept the Mosiac law (think Leviticus), in addition to believing in Jesus, they would receive a "better" salvation. The holier the life, the better they appeared before God.

Paul reminds the Galatians that to live by the Law only brings death and condemnation. He quotes Deuteronomy 27:26 to show that one must keep the whole Law to gain acceptance by God. The Law requires perfection, which no one can attain. Faith in Jesus is all that's needed for salvation, and anyone can exercise faith.

PARTICIPANT GUIDE

What is God communicating to us by removing all requirements other than faith in Christ for our salvation?

INTERESTING THOUGHTS SPARKED BY OTHERS IN MY GROUP:

BEHIND THE SCENES

When Paul calls the Galatians "foolish," he's not calling them stupid or ignorant. The word he uses for "foolish" is *anoētos*, which refers to someone who is irrational or fails to use the intellect they have. This is a person who can think but isn't using what they know and have experienced to discern the truth. As an example he says that "Jesus Christ was clearly portrayed among you as crucified." "Clearly portrayed" literally means "to write for public reading." It's as if it was posted on billboards everywhere. Paul had made Christ's crucifixion so clear and understandable that for the Galatians to turn from it and embrace the Law as part of salvation, Paul could only count this as "foolish" or as if the Galatians had been bewitched.

What is enticing about making ourselves look better for God? Is it really for God that we're doing these things?

BEHIND THE SCENES

While the Judaizers were focused on Moses and the Law God had given him, Paul refers the Galatians to Abraham, who lived hundreds of years prior to the Mosaic law. He reminds them that "Abraham believed the Lord, and he credited it to him as righteousness" (Genesis 15:6). Abraham wasn't considered righteous before God because he obeyed God and was circumcised but because he believed God. Notice Abraham didn't simply believe *in* God, as many do, but he believed God. He trusted God. Paul is saying that knowledge of God and following a set of rules isn't what saves. Instead, trusting who Jesus says he is and what he can do makes one righteous.

GROWING

What about your life? Do you find yourself striving to do things that, even subconsciously, might make God smile on you? To earn his blessing or favor? Or have you found freedom in living by faith in Jesus? How would your relationship with God be different if you truly did simply live by faith in the forgiveness and acceptance of Christ?

Write your personal response here.

LESSON 4: WHAT DOES A LIFE OF FREEDOM LOOK LIKE?

GREETING

How do you define freedom?

What are a few ways you exercise your freedom each day?

GROUNDING

God's Word: Galatians 5:1-15

[1] It is for freedom that Christ has set us free. Stand firm, then, and do not let yourselves be burdened again by a yoke of slavery.

[2] Mark my words! I, Paul, tell you that if you let yourselves be circumcised, Christ will be of no value to you at all. [3] Again I declare to every man who lets himself be circumcised that he is obligated to obey the whole law. [4] You who are trying to be justified by the law have been alienated from Christ; you have fallen away from grace. [5] For through the Spirit we eagerly await by faith the righteousness for which we hope. [6] For in Christ Jesus neither circumcision nor uncircumcision has any value. The only thing that counts is faith expressing itself through love.

[7] You were running a good race. Who cut in on you to keep you from obeying the truth? [8] That kind of persuasion does not come from the one who calls you. [9] "A little yeast works through the whole batch of dough." [10] I am confident in the Lord that you will take no other view. The one who is throwing you into confusion, whoever that may be, will have to pay the penalty. [11] Brothers and sisters, if I am still preaching circumcision, why am I still being persecuted? In that case the offense of the cross has been abolished. [12] As for those agitators, I wish they would go the whole way and emasculate themselves!

[13] You, my brothers and sisters, were called to be free. But do not use your freedom to indulge the flesh; rather, serve one another humbly in love. [14] For the entire law is fulfilled in keeping this one command: "Love your neighbor as yourself." [15] If you bite and devour each other, watch out or you will be destroyed by each other.

What are the first questions that come to mind? What words or phrases catch your attention?

Capture your initial thoughts and questions here.

BEHIND THE SCENES

Paul directly addressed the issue of circumcision, because it was causing a divide between Gentile Christians (non-Jews) and Judaizers. Judaizers were Jewish Christians who insisted that Gentile Christians must live like Jews, submitting to all Jewish laws. As Jewish people accepted Jesus as the Messiah, they continued to keep the laws that had been part of their heritage. Circumcision was a sign of the covenant between God and the Jewish people. Judaizers could not fathom anyone following God without following these kinds of rules and practices. But Paul insisted Jesus had made a new way for both Jews and Gentiles to become part of God's family and to live in the freedom God offered.

This is what Paul meant when he warned the Galatians about "trying to be justified by the law." Following the Jewish law would not count for anything on the day of judgment, when God, the judge of the whole world, would declare who was in the right and part of God's family. That future declaration has been activated in the present on the basis of Jesus' death on the cross. The means of receiving this present justification now is faith. Those who believe in Jesus don't have to wait for their judgment; they are already "justified." Because of this gracious decision, both Jews and Gentiles who are in Christ are full members of God's people!

GRAPPLING

GOING DEEPER

Some questions are left unanswered, which often makes us uncomfortable. Inquiring minds want to know, and we want to know now! Sometimes we're curious and want to learn to grow, but other times we're just nosy. Truth is, none of us have, or need, all the answers or all the information. Questions are good when the motivation behind them is good. Commit to checking your motivation and accepting that you'll never have all the answers. That kind of knowledge and understanding is reserved for God.

BEHIND THE SCENES

Paul said, "You were running a good race. Who cut in on you to keep you from obeying the truth? That kind of persuasion does not come from the one who calls you" (Galatians 5:7-8). Just because we start well doesn't mean we finish well. We can blame God, saying he isn't giving us what we need. But just because God has authority over all things doesn't mean our lives are free from all other forces and influences. In the case of the Galatians, Paul was referring to the Jewish Christians who challenged the Galatians' spiritual growth. The Galatians weren't fully living in the freedom they had, because they were letting other people limit and control their spiritual lives.

What are some influences and forces that limit our sense of freedom?

Which of these forces are self-imposed and which are imposed from outside ourselves?

How can uncontrolled freedom lead to conflict and disunity between people?

INTERESTING THOUGHTS SPARKED BY OTHERS IN MY GROUP:

BEHIND THE SCENES

Paul often taught about freedom, including the responsible use of it. In 1 Corinthians 10:23, he said, "'I have the right to do anything,' you say—but not everything is beneficial. 'I have the right to do anything'—but not everything is constructive." He quoted a statement that contains truth but shouldn't be misapplied with self-centered rationalizations. Yes, freedom implies rights, but just because we have freedom doesn't mean we should use it the way we want to in every situation. Paul cautioned to take care that "the exercise of your rights does not become a stumbling block to the weak" (1 Corinthians 8:9). Freedom involves humble consideration of and service to others.

GROWING

BEHIND THE SCENES

Paul's admonition to "love your neighbor as yourself" is a reference to Leviticus 19:18. When Jesus was asked to identify the greatest commandment, he included loving others as the second part, following, "Love the Lord your God with all your heart and with all your soul and with all your mind" (Matthew 22:36-40). In the Leviticus passage, the commandment to love your neighbor as yourself is in the context of God's people being holy because he is holy. God's instruction begins with who he is, and then expands to who we are and how we are to respond because of who he is. We love others because it honors God.

What corrections might you need to make to fully live with freedom?

Write those thoughts here.

What do you anticipate or hope will be noticeable differences as you embrace the fullness of living a life of freedom?

Capture those ideas here.

LESSON 5: HOW CAN I GET ALONG WITH OTHERS— EVEN WHEN I DON'T FEEL LIKE IT?

GREETING

What do others do that you find annoying?

Your group has been hired by a company to create some guidelines for helping people get along in that company. Circle the type of company you are assigned from the list below:

- children's amusement park
- nursing home
- monster truck rally
- small manned spacecraft
- cooking class
- summer camp
- buffet restaurant
- scientific research tent in Antarctica

As a group, come up with a few guidelines, standards, or rules to keep everyone safe, healthy, and happy in your assigned setting.

Write your group's guidelines here.

What issues did you consider when creating your list of guidelines?

Which of those issues were most important and which issues were of lower priority?

GROUNDING

God's Word: 1 Thessalonians 5:12-22

[12] Now we ask you, brothers and sisters, to acknowledge those who work hard among you, who care for you in the Lord and who admonish you. [13] Hold them in the highest regard in love because of their work. Live in peace with each other. [14] And we urge you, brothers and sisters, warn those who are idle and disruptive, encourage the disheartened, help the weak, be patient with everyone. [15] Make sure that nobody pays back wrong for wrong, but always strive to do what is good for each other and for everyone else.

[16] Rejoice always, [17] pray continually, [18] give thanks in all circumstances; for this is God's will for you in Christ Jesus.

[19] Do not quench the Spirit. [20] Do not treat prophecies with contempt [21] but test them all; hold on to what is good, [22] reject every kind of evil.

BEHIND THE SCENES

The Apostle Paul wrote two letters to the church in Thessalonica. The city was named by Cassander, king of Macedonia, a small kingdom in what is today northeastern Greece. He honored his wife, Thessalonike—a stepsister of Alexander the Great—by naming the city after her. He invested in making the city stronger and larger. Later, the Romans turned Macedonia into one of their provinces, with Thessalonica being the most important city. It had a harbor and was a major stop on the Egnatian Road, a main highway through the Roman world.

This made Thessalonica a strategically sound place for the Apostle Paul to preach the Gospel and establish a church. The church in Thessalonica could, and did, have influence throughout Macedonia and other parts of the Roman Empire. It was composed mostly of Gentiles rather than Jews, and it became one of the strongest churches Paul planted.

What are the first questions that come to mind? What words or phrases catch your attention?

Write those initial thoughts and questions here.

GRAPPLING

GOING DEEPER

Bible passages like the one covered in this lesson use short, simple sentences that can sound like they're describing simple concepts. But these concepts can be difficult to understand and even more difficult to live by. Don't worry if you don't have it all figured out and your life doesn't reflect these requirements all the time—no one's does! The important thing is that as we welcome Christ and submit to the work of the Holy Spirit in our lives, he will make us more like the people he wants us to be. Acknowledging we don't have it all together is really the first step—and that can start in this class. As you do so, you'll be making it a safe place for everyone to be honest about their shortcomings and ultimately about their need for Jesus.

BEHIND THE SCENES

Paul's instructions to "warn those who are idle and disruptive, encourage the disheartened, help the weak, be patient with everyone" reflect military terminology. The words described soldiers who are 1) unruly or out of order; 2) timid or discouraged in the face of the enemy; 3) weak or vulnerable to attack.

This is in keeping with passages such as Ephesians 6:10-20 and 2 Timothy 2:1-6, which compare the Christian life to battle and Christians themselves to soldiers engaged in the fight. The three different types of soldiers require different responses from others.

At the same time, his instruction to "be patient with everyone" (verse 14) is not at all specific. It applies to all. Every one of us requires patience at various times in our lives, and we all owe it to each other.

If we, as Christians, have God's Spirit living in us, why don't we always get along?

How can we "warn" idle and disruptive people while at the same time hold them in high regard and live in peace with them?

INTERESTING THOUGHTS SPARKED BY OTHERS IN MY GROUP:

BEHIND THE SCENES

First Thessalonians 5:18 can be easily misunderstood. Paul's words to "give thanks in all circumstances" do not mean we must thank God when tragedy or misfortune comes our way, for not all these events come from God. But because God is present with us in any and all circumstances—including the bad ones—we can give thanks for that presence. Paul calls Christians to give thanks *in* all circumstances, not necessarily *for* all circumstances.

According to this passage, what qualities and actions should we apply to get along with each other?

PARTICIPANT GUIDE

GROWING

Find one partner, and then pick one of the instructions in these verses that suggests a way you need to grow in order to better get along with other people. Maybe you need to exercise more patience with others. Maybe you need to help the weak or stop paying back others with wrong for wrong. Tell your partner what you've chosen, and write down that commitment below. Then pray together for God's help to change your heart and life for greater harmony with others.

Write your commitment here.

LESSON 6: IS MY PASTOR BETTER THAN YOUR PASTOR?

GREETING

With your group, design your own superhero according to the criteria below.

Your hero's name: _____

Your hero's superpowers: _____

Why is your superhero the best? _____

Why should a kid want to grow up to be just like your character?

Why is your superhero worth following above all others?

Why do you think so many people identify with a particular superhero (and if not a superhero, a feisty and empowered Disney princess or similar character)?

Who are some well-known Christian leaders in our culture whom many people admire?

What good can come from Christian leaders being widely respected and followed?

And what are some of the dangers of putting our church leaders on a pedestal?

GROUNDING

God's Word: 1 Corinthians 1:10-17; 3:4-9

¹⁰ I appeal to you, brothers and sisters, in the name of our Lord Jesus Christ, that all of you agree with one another in what you say and that there be no divisions among you, but that you be perfectly united in ▶

mind and thought. [11] My brothers and sisters, some from Chloe's household have informed me that there are quarrels among you. [12] What I mean is this: One of you says, "I follow Paul"; another, "I follow Apollos"; another, "I follow Cephas"; still another, "I follow Christ."

[13] Is Christ divided? Was Paul crucified for you? Were you baptized in the name of Paul? [14] I thank God that I did not baptize any of you except Crispus and Gaius, [15] so no one can say that you were baptized in my name. [16] (Yes, I also baptized the household of Stephanas; beyond that, I don't remember if I baptized anyone else.) [17] For Christ did not send me to baptize, but to preach the gospel—not with wisdom and eloquence, lest the cross of Christ be emptied of its power.

[4] For when one says, "I follow Paul," and another, "I follow Apollos," are you not mere human beings?

[5] What, after all, is Apollos? And what is Paul? Only servants, through whom you came to believe—as the Lord has assigned to each his task. [6] I planted the seed, Apollos watered it, but God has been making it grow. [7] So neither the one who plants nor the one who waters is anything, but only God, who makes things grow. [8] The one who plants and the one who waters have one purpose, and they will each be rewarded according to their own labor. [9] For we are co-workers in God's service; you are God's field, God's building.

As we read this passage, what were the first questions that came to mind? What do you make of the issues that threatened to divide the Corinthian church?

Record your initial thoughts and questions here.

BEHIND THE SCENES

Paul had his hands full with the Corinthian church. The two letters he wrote to them are filled with numerous warnings and corrections. The church tolerated sexual immorality among family members. They abused the Lord's Supper and turned it into a showy social event that showcased the church's wealthiest members. They took each other to court instead of making an attempt at reconciliation. They started to collect money to combat the poverty in Jerusalem but then lost interest.

In our passage, Paul dealt with the Corinthians' tendency to get into heated arguments over their spiritual leaders. The text mentions three strong leaders who invested themselves in the life of the Corinthian church. Paul founded the church during his second missionary journey. Sometime after that, Apollos, a preacher from Alexandria, moved to Corinth and ministered to the church after Paul left. The city of Alexandria was one of the cultural and intellectual hubs of the Roman Empire. It's likely that Apollos would have been exposed to the ideas and speaking style of the famous Greek teacher, Philo. This potentially gave Apollos a highly polished speaking style. The Apostle Peter (the Cephas in verse 12) apparently had a hand in the development of the Corinthian church, although we're unclear as to what his role was.

Instead of being grateful for the wealth of leaders God provided them, the Corinthians debated which of these three leaders most influenced their faith. Each camp picked a leader to venerate while dismissing the value of the other two. Paul's letter doesn't explain how such a disagreement came to be. Even though Paul had some disputes with Peter (see Galatians 2), he didn't nurse old grudges to gain sympathy. Instead, Paul focused his attention on the source of their unity: Jesus Christ. He is the one who reconciles all people to himself. Paul challenged the people to return to the basis of their unity and regain their dignity as God's people.

GRAPPLING

BEHIND THE SCENES

Even though the Corinthian church was displaying spiritually immature behavior, Paul used two metaphors to gently remind them of their dignity. He first told them (in 1 Corinthians 3:6-17) they were God's carefully groomed field that was just waiting to bear fruit. Then he reminded them that collectively they were God's building—the temple. The first metaphor served a few purposes. Paul used it to remind them that just as it takes more than one person to work a field, God used a number of "farmers" to cultivate their church. None of these workers possessed the gift of life that would create the yield. The metaphor also implied they were to bear a better fruit than the divisive arguments they were currently yielding.

The metaphor of God's temple reminded them of their interconnectedness in Christ. No single brick by itself offers anything of value. However, when the building materials are arranged in such a way that they are interconnected with each other, a strong structure can be built. They needed each other, and they needed the contribution of each church leader.

Why do you think Paul appealed to them "in the name of our Lord Jesus Christ"? How might remembering Jesus make it hard to maintain their current positions?

How do you think our modern church culture's obsession with celebrity pastors is the same as the Corinthians' obsession? How is it different?

How can we keep our appreciation for a particular pastor or leader from deteriorating into unhealthy hero worship?

GOING DEEPER

The Corinthians learned everyone's contribution was needed for the church to thrive. Look around the room. Is there anyone in the room who seems hesitant to share? Look for opportunities to ask that person for their opinion. Or thank them when they do share.

BEHIND THE SCENES

Paul wanted the Corinthians to be of one mind, but he wasn't asking them to agree on everything. He wasn't condemning their differences of opinions. He was addressing their lack of respect and solidarity as they disagreed. Instead of getting tangled up in the details of their argument, he knew the best course of action was to keep pointing them back to Jesus.

INTERESTING THOUGHTS SPARKED BY OTHERS IN MY GROUP:

GROWING

What questions could I ask myself to keep me from turning my interest in a speaker or author into something unhealthy?

Write your thoughts here.

What are some ways I could express my disagreement with a "celebrity pastor" without disparaging them as a Christian and as a person?

Write your ideas here.

LESSON 7: HOW FAR CAN I TAKE GOD'S GRACE?

GREETING

If Michael were to insist that he's an adult and free to do whatever he pleases, how would you respond to him?

What are some areas of life where people can take a good thing and overindulge or engage in it excessively?

In many of these cases, the root problem is that people let their short-term desires overrule their long-term goals. Why do you think that's so easy to do?

GROUNDING

God's Word: 1 Corinthians 6:12-20

[12] "I have the right to do anything," you say—but not everything is beneficial. "I have the right to do anything"—but I will not be mastered by anything. [13] You say, "Food for the stomach and the stomach for food, and God will destroy them both." The body, however, is not meant for sexual immorality but for the Lord, and the Lord for the body. [14] By his power God raised the Lord from the dead, and he will raise us also. [15] Do you not know that your bodies are members of Christ himself? Shall I then take the members of Christ and unite them with a prostitute? Never! [16] Do you not know that he who unites himself with a prostitute is one with her in body? For it is said, "The two will become one flesh." [17] But whoever is united with the Lord is one with him in spirit.

[18] Flee from sexual immorality. All other sins a person commits are outside the body, but whoever sins sexually, sins against their own body. [19] Do you not know that your bodies are temples of the Holy Spirit, who is in you, whom you have received from God? You are not your own; [20] you were bought at a price. Therefore honor God with your bodies.

What are the first questions that come to mind? What words or phrases stand out to you as important?

Write down your thoughts and questions here.

PARTICIPANT GUIDE

BEHIND THE SCENES

Of all the churches the Apostle Paul cared for, the Corinthian congregation was the messiest, morally speaking. In today's passage, Paul found himself having to deal with a pair of calamitous errors in this congregation. Corinth was a pagan city (and a notoriously wicked seaport, to boot), and as such it didn't subscribe to God's standards regarding sexual expression. Apparently, many of the new converts didn't understand that sex outside the context of marriage was sinful. And they simultaneously misunderstood Paul's teaching on God's grace and Christian liberty. Paul had railed against legalism with one-liners like, "It is for freedom that Christ has set us free. Stand firm then and do not let yourselves be burdened again by a yoke of slavery" (Galatians 5:1). Along these same lines, the Corinthians were fond of saying, "I have the right to do anything." They may have learned that slogan from Paul himself; however, they removed it from its proper context and took it to extremes.

So, Paul found himself having to instruct the Corinthians that these sayings were true regarding any particular behavior only when balanced by considering the consequences in light of God's purposes. God's grace wasn't "carte blanche" that allowed them to do whatever they wanted with their bodies. God's design for humans had—and still has—a long-range goal to restore all of creation to its original pure and innocent condition. That includes the human body.

GOING DEEPER

"Everything is permissible, but not everything is beneficial" is a great filter for us to use as we choose our words during fearless conversations. Be sure to choose words that encourage others, draw them into the conversation, and add to everyone's collective understanding of the passage.

GRAPPLING

BEHIND THE SCENES

Paul could have led by saying, "Fornication is a sin: Stop it!" But he wanted to do more than merely give a lesson in Morality 101. He wanted to teach them something about the Christian view of the body. So he started by adding a qualifier to their pet motto about freedom. "Yes, I'm 'allowed to do anything'—but not everything I do is to my advantage." It would have been difficult for the Corinthians to disagree with that.

The second pet saying, about food and the stomach, was being used as an excuse for sexual immorality. If the stomach was made for food and food for the stomach, they extended that analogy as if to say that the body was made for sex, and sex was designed for the body. Paul didn't deny that God created humans as sexual beings, but he did insist that God's purpose is not fulfilled by any and all sexual practices.

Paul's argument rested on the assumption that sexual intercourse is more than a physical act. Borrowing language from the Genesis story of Adam and Eve, Paul stated that a sexual encounter creates a physical *and* spiritual union between the two parties—they become "one flesh." Humans, including our physical bodies, were made for the Lord, and as such are inhabited by God's Spirit. We weren't designed as discrete, unrelated parts of body, soul, and spirit. Rather, we exist as an integrated whole. So sexual choices do matter, and excessive abuse of our bodies in this arena will have an adverse effect on all our other relationships.

PARTICIPANT GUIDE

Paul reminded the Corinthians that their bodies were designed to honor God. In what ways does knowing our God-given purpose help avoid taking advantage of God's free grace?

What do you think about Paul's view of the human person as a unity of body and spirit? What does this mean for other human interactions besides sexual practices?

INTERESTING THOUGHTS SPARKED BY OTHERS IN MY GROUP:

The temple in Jerusalem was special to the Jews of Paul's day. It represented the one earthly dwelling place for God's personal presence. What do you think Paul implied about our bodies by calling them "temples of the Holy Spirit"?

What does the "high price" that God bought us at tell us about our value to him? How could this motivate us in how we choose to use our bodies?

GROWING

Is the way I've been using my freedom in Christ helping me fulfill God's purpose for me?

Capture those thoughts here.

How well do I appreciate the value God places on me—body and spirit? How could that knowledge change my attitudes and behavior?

Write those reflections here.

PARTICIPANT GUIDE

LESSON 8: WHERE DO I FIT IN THE BODY OF CHRIST?

GREETING

How might the lessons we learned from the movie quiz we took be applied to the topic of our place in the body of Christ?

What do you think would be the most difficult body part to adjust to losing suddenly? Explain your answer.

What body part do you think you could most easily learn to get along without?

GROUNDING

God's Word: 1 Corinthians 12:12-31

[12] Just as a body, though one, has many parts, but all its many parts form one body, so it is with Christ. [13] For we were all baptized by one Spirit so as to form one body—whether Jews or Gentiles, slave or free—and we were all given the one Spirit to drink. [14] Even so the body is not made up of one part but of many.

[15] Now if the foot should say, "Because I am not a hand, I do not belong to the body," it would not for that reason stop being part of the body. [16] And if the ear should say, "Because I am not an eye, I do not belong to the body," it would not for that reason stop being part of the body. [17] If the whole body were an eye, where would the sense of hearing be? If the whole body were an ear, where would the sense of smell be? [18] But in fact God has placed the parts in the body, every one of them, just as he wanted them to be. [19] If they were all one part, where would the body be? [20] As it is, there are many parts, but one body.

PARTICIPANT GUIDE

▼

[21] The eye cannot say to the hand, "I don't need you!" And the head cannot say to the feet, "I don't need you!" [22] On the contrary, those parts of the body that seem to be weaker are indispensable, [23] and the parts that we think are less honorable we treat with special honor. And the parts that are unpresentable are treated with special modesty, [24] while our presentable parts need no special treatment. But God has put the body together, giving greater honor to the parts that lacked it, [25] so that there should be no division in the body, but that its parts should have equal concern for each other. [26] If one part suffers, every part suffers with it; if one part is honored, every part rejoices with it.

[27] Now you are the body of Christ, and each one of you is a part of it. [28] And God has placed in the church first of all apostles, second prophets, third teachers, then miracles, then gifts of healing, of helping, of guidance, and of different kinds of tongues. [29] Are all apostles? Are all prophets? Are all teachers? Do all work miracles? [30] Do all have gifts of healing? Do all speak in tongues? Do all interpret? [31] Now eagerly desire the greater gifts. And yet I will show you the most excellent way.

What are the first questions that come to mind? What ideas, words, or phrases catch your attention?

Write your initial thoughts and questions here.

GRAPPLING

GOING DEEPER

You can help others in your group go deeper by listening with your full attention and by asking questions as others share. Saying "I wonder about what you just said. Tell me more!" will help people know you care about what they're saying and want them to open up more.

BEHIND THE SCENES

Corinth is a city about 48 miles west of Athens, which Paul visited around A.D. 52. Corinth was a large city whose geography made it a profitable trading center between Asia and Italy. Corinthians were also familiar with the classic Greek philosophers, such as Socrates and Aristotle, and enjoyed gathering to debate issues and the pursuit of "wisdom." Mostly, though, Corinth was known for sensuality and immorality. One temple in the city devoted to the goddess of love, Aphrodite, provided "employment" for 10,000 prostitutes.

Paul visited Corinth and became friends with Pricilla and Aquilla, two tentmakers who ultimately became leaders of the Corinthian church. He wrote the letter of 1 Corinthians from Ephesus around A.D. 56, when the church was about 4 years old, to address issues that had arisen in the time since Paul had left Corinth.

Who would people in your church say is the most indispensible member of your church? What would your answer be if you didn't include the pastor as a possibility?

What would our church—or the global church—look like if each member participated as God intended the church to function?

INTERESTING THOUGHTS SPARKED BY OTHERS IN MY GROUP:

BEHIND THE SCENES

When Paul wrote, "whether Jews or Gentiles, slave or free," it's as if he said, "whether American or European, rich or poor." Nationality, denomination, and social standing are inconsequential to Jesus. Everyone who believes in him is "baptized," or made a part of his body through the Holy Spirit, and is necessary to its function. Additionally, when Paul wrote, "we were all given one Spirit to drink," he was indicating that the Holy Spirit dwells in each believer, just as the water you drink enters your body and gives life.

How might a desire for personal praise and consideration hurt the church?

BEHIND THE SCENES

Apparently, the Corinthian church had placed higher value on some people in their church, based upon what they could do. But Paul asserted that no one person was more valuable than any other. In fact, verse 28 contains a short list of gifts and abilities that is arranged in reverse order of their seeming importance to the Corinthian church. While those who could speak in tongues or perform healings were seen as more important by the Corinthians, Paul listed apostles, prophets, and teachers first! In light of the entire passage, Paul was not saying these three are more important, but all are equally necessary to the church.

GROWING

BEHIND THE SCENES

The word for gifts in verse 28 is *charisma*, meaning favor or gift. The root of this word is *charis*, which means grace. When put together it indicates something that is graciously given. Spiritual gifts are not earned but graciously given to each person by God.

What about you? Where do you fit? Maybe you feel like an extra in the background of a movie and it leaves you feeling not so important. Or do you know where you fit and enjoy using your graciously given gift? Reflect on the passions and gifts God has given you, and journal your thoughts to God.

Journal those thoughts here.

LESSON 9: HOW CAN I GET THROUGH THE HARD TIMES IN LIFE?

GREETING

What do you think separates the people who show resilience under pressure and those who wilt or are crushed by pressure?

How does what's going on around me (external events) define and affect the hard times in life?

How does what's going on inside me (internal thoughts, attitudes, and feelings) define and affect the hard times in life?

GROUNDING

God's Word: 2 Corinthians 4:5-18

[5] For what we preach is not ourselves, but Jesus Christ as Lord, and ourselves as your servants for Jesus' sake. [6] For God, who said, "Let light shine out of darkness," made his light shine in our hearts to give us the light of the knowledge of God's glory displayed in the face of Christ.

[7] But we have this treasure in jars of clay to show that this all-surpassing power is from God and not from us. [8] We are hard pressed on every side, but not crushed; perplexed, but not in despair; [9] persecuted, but not abandoned; struck down, but not destroyed. [10] We always carry around in our body the death of Jesus, so that the life of Jesus may also be revealed in our body. [11] For we who are alive are always being given over to death for Jesus' sake, so that his life may also be revealed in our mortal body. [12] So then, death is at work in us, but life is at work in you.

[13] It is written: "I believed; therefore I have spoken." Since we have that same spirit of faith, we also believe and therefore speak, [14] because we know that the one who raised the Lord Jesus from the dead will also raise us with Jesus and present us with you to himself. [15] All this is for your benefit, so that the grace that is reaching more and more people may cause thanksgiving to overflow to the glory of God.

[16] Therefore we do not lose heart. Though outwardly we are wasting away, yet inwardly we are being renewed day by day. [17] For our light and momentary troubles are achieving for us an eternal glory that far outweighs them all. [18] So we fix our eyes not on what is seen, but on what is unseen, since what is seen is temporary, but what is unseen is eternal.

What in this passage catches your attention or spurs a question?

Write those initial thoughts and questions here.

GRAPPLING

GOING DEEPER

Each of us has experienced hurt of some kind. God created us for relationships, which can, themselves, create hard times for us. However, we can also rely on each other during the hard times. In order to do so, we need to build healthy relationships when we're not in crisis, when we have the time and energy to invest in growing relationships. When we do, we invite others into our lives and we share the burdens. Only God can carry us through the crises of our lives, but he often brings people alongside us to be his hands and feet, as well as to provide a listening ear and encouraging tongue that speaks God's truth. Invest in relationships that honor God today in preparation for tomorrow.

BEHIND THE SCENES

Hard times often make us feel ill-equipped or weak. However, because of Jesus' death and resurrection, what looks like weakness and humiliation actually comes with the promise of power. The Cross wasn't about passive suffering; it was about the power in suffering for the sake of others, which can be redemptive. Suffering also allows us to identify with Jesus. If we hope to experience the new life of resurrection now, in this life, we must be prepared to see crucifixion at work as well. But if we can hold onto our faith in suffering, we will ultimately experience the final resurrection when we live forever with Jesus.

What does being a servant for Jesus' sake involve when you're going through hard times?

In hard times, what *challenges* you about setting your eyes on what is unseen instead of what is seen?

In hard times, what *encourages* you about setting your eyes on what is unseen instead of what is seen?

BEHIND THE SCENES

Paul repeatedly uses opposites to show the vast difference between human frailty or mortality and God's power. In 2 Corinthians 4:8-9, the opposites include: hard pressed on every side versus not crushed, perplexed versus not in despair, persecuted versus not abandoned, and struck down versus not destroyed. In each case, we feel as if we really *are* being crushed, in despair, abandoned, or destroyed. But despite what we experience in our humanness, the mysterious power of God allows us to persevere and come out the other side stronger than before. God shows us mercy and gives us hope that Jesus' resurrected life will be at work in us. In verses 17-18, Paul expressed his confidence that God's true reality will one day take full effect and we will enjoy God's presence without limits.

In everyday life, especially in the hard times, what does not giving up look like? Be specific!

PARTICIPANT GUIDE

BEHIND THE SCENES

Although we might not like to face it, the Bible includes multiple references about God's people experiencing suffering and distress (John 16:33; Acts 14:22; Romans 5:3; 2 Corinthians 4:17; Revelation 2:10). Earthly sufferings are temporary. We give up our lives to live God's way. As we do, God works life into us. Second Corinthians 4:12 says, "Death is at work in us." The Greek word used for "at work in" is *energēs*. It means to cause something to happen. It's active. Perhaps you can see the English word "energy" or "energize" in it. Just as Jesus' death worked to overcome the power of sin and death in the world, our sufferings can lead to "an eternal glory that far outweighs them all" (verse 17).

GROWING

BEHIND THE SCENES

When we, or someone we know, are going through hard times, we often hear the soothing reminder that God doesn't give us more than we can handle. The verses often quoted—or misquoted—are 1 Corinthians 10:12-13: "So, if you think you are standing firm, be careful that you don't fall! No temptation has overtaken you except what is common to mankind. And God is faithful; he will not let you be tempted beyond what you can bear. But when you are tempted, he will also provide a way out so that you can endure it."

Although these verses might be intended to sooth us in moments of hardship, it's not really appropriate in that context. These verses address temptations, not the more general category of burdens or hard times. (Plus, even when we are tempted, God promises to provide a way out, not to remove the temptation.) Hardships are bound to come, and the Bible gives us no guarantee God will lead us out of them. But the Bible does assure us that God is with us and will be faithful to renew us day by day (2 Corinthians 4:16). Our choice lies in whether or not we fix our eyes on the unseen, eternal glory that is promised. What will be your response when hard times hit?

What have I learned about getting through the hard times in life?

Write those thoughts here.

How am I going to respond in fearless faith today?

Capture your ideas here.

LESSON 10: WHY SHOULD I BE GENEROUS WHEN OTHERS HAVE MORE THAN I DO?

GREETING

If you had $100,000 to give to a charity, what charity would you want to benefit, and what would you want that money to be used for?

If you had $10 to give to a charity, what charity would you want to benefit, and what would you want the money to be used for?

Was it more satisfying for you to imagine giving away $100,000 or $10? Why?

When you hear about people who are in a position to give astronomical amounts to benefit the common good, are you motivated to increase your level of generosity? Or are you discouraged? Or are you indifferent? Why?

GROUNDING

God's Word: 2 Corinthians 8:1-15

[1] And now, brothers and sisters, we want you to know about the grace that God has given the Macedonian churches. [2] In the midst of a very severe trial, their overflowing joy and their extreme poverty welled up in rich generosity. [3] For I testify that they gave as much as they were able, and even beyond their ability. Entirely on their own, [4] they urgently pleaded with us for the privilege of sharing in this service to the Lord's people. [5] And they exceeded our expectations: They gave themselves first of all to the Lord, and then by the will of God also to us. [6] So we urged Titus, just as he had earlier made a beginning, to bring also to completion this act of grace on your part. [7] But since you excel in everything—in faith, in speech, in knowledge, in complete earnestness and in the love we have kindled in you—see that you also excel in this grace of giving.

[8] I am not commanding you, but I want to test the sincerity of your love by comparing it with the earnestness of others. [9] For you know the grace

of our Lord Jesus Christ, that though he was rich, yet for your sake he became poor, so that you through his poverty might become rich.

[10] And here is my judgment about what is best for you in this matter. Last year you were the first not only to give but also to have the desire to do so. [11] Now finish the work, so that your eager willingness to do it may be matched by your completion of it, according to your means. [12] For if the willingness is there, the gift is acceptable according to what one has, not according to what one does not have.

[13] Our desire is not that others might be relieved while you are hard pressed, but that there might be equality. [14] At the present time your plenty will supply what they need, so that in turn their plenty will supply what you need. The goal is equality, [15] as it is written: "The one who gathered much did not have too much, and the one who gathered little did not have too little."

What are the first questions that come to mind? What strikes you about this passage?

Record your initial thoughts and questions here.

BEHIND THE SCENES

Around A.D. 45 the church in Jerusalem fell into deep poverty. This might have been the result of the fierce persecution that was sparked by the stoning of Stephen (Acts 11:19), or the great famine that much of the known world was experiencing (Acts 11:28), or a combination of the two. Paul mobilized multiple churches to participate in the offering to the Jerusalem church, writing to the Roman Christians (Romans 15:26-36), the Galatians (Galatians 2:10), and the Corinthians (1 Corinthians 16:1-4). In the passage we're studying this lesson, Paul mentions the churches in Macedonia as having contributed generously to this collection. (Macedonia was the name of the Roman province in the northern part of Greece and included the churches at Philippi, Berea, and the provincial capital of Thessalonica.)

In his first letter to the Corinthians, Paul gave detailed instructions for the church to take up a collection for their Jerusalem brothers and sisters (1 Corinthians 16:1-3). The Corinthians had begun to collect money but then lost interest or changed their minds and discontinued the collection. In today's passage, Paul appealed to the Corinthians to resume the collection offering as evidence of their unity with other Christians and their love for Christ.

GRAPPLING

BEHIND THE SCENES

Paul had several motives for relieving the poverty that afflicted the Jerusalem Christians. When the apostles commissioned him to minister to the Gentiles, they gave him specific instructions to "remember the poor" (Galatians 2:10). Paul also saw the offering as a way to ease tensions between the Jewish Christians and the Gentile Christians by providing tangible evidence of their unity in Christ. But mostly, Paul viewed the offering as an opportunity to demonstrate their love for God and others. At no point did Paul discuss budgets or giving amounts. Instead, he spoke to the Corinthians theologically, so they could understand he was presenting them with an opportunity for spiritual growth. He called the ability to participate in the offering a form of grace—a privilege. The offering itself is called a "ministry." It appears he believed that if the Corinthians understood this, the amount of money would take care of itself.

GOING DEEPER

Be sensitive as you share. Giving and finances can be a difficult subject for some people. Avoid making statements that might be misconstrued as being judgmental. Instead, consider taking a risk and sharing a struggle you've had with becoming generous. Who knows, you might spark some real, authentic sharing!

What precautions did Paul take to make sure the Corinthians didn't feel obligated to give? What opportunities would Paul have robbed them of if he "laid down the law" and ordered them to participate in the offering?

What do you see as the connection between being generous with our money and our spiritual health?

INTERESTING THOUGHTS SPARKED BY OTHERS IN MY GROUP:

Why do you think the attitude of the giver matters more than the amount given? Or...do you think that's true at all?

BEHIND THE SCENES

Paul was a master of public relations in this passage. Although he had severely criticized the Corinthians in other parts of his letters to them, here Paul lavished the compliments. He told them they excelled in faith, speech, knowledge, earnestness, and love (verse 7). He also offered his advice as just that, advice, rather than as a command. Most notably, Paul compared the Corinthians to the Macedonian churches, who had given more than they were realistically able to do. He may have been taking advantage of regional rivalries, for Macedonia was the Roman province in the northern part of Greece. Corinth, on the other hand, was the capital of the southern Greek province of Achaia, which also included the city of Athens. The crowning touch of Paul's rhetoric is to compare the Corinthians to their Lord Jesus Christ, who, though he was rich, became poor for their sakes. How could anyone be stingy in light of such an incomparable gift?

PARTICIPANT GUIDE

GROWING

How are you personally challenged by the topic of this lesson? What might you do differently as a result of this conversation?

Write those ideas here.

Who is someone you could personally bless with even a small gift? What would it take for you to make that happen?

Write your thoughts here.

LESSON 11:
SHOULDN'T PEOPLE CLEAN UP BEFORE THEY COME TO GOD?

GREETING

What is the dirtiest job you have ever had to do?

What have you found to be the best products and practices that work on cleaning filthy dirty clothes/hands/body?

When we meet someone new or important, or when we have company visit our home, what different or special things do we do to clean up before meeting them? Why do we go to all this effort?

P A R T I C I P A N T   G U I D E

GROUNDING

God's Word: Romans 5:1-11

[1] Therefore, since we have been justified through faith, we have peace with God through our Lord Jesus Christ, [2] through whom we have gained access by faith into this grace in which we now stand. And we boast in the hope of the glory of God. [3] Not only so, but we also glory in our sufferings, because we know that suffering produces perseverance; [4] perseverance, character; and character, hope. [5] And hope does not put us to shame, because God's love has been poured out into our hearts through the Holy Spirit, who has been given to us.

[6] You see, at just the right time, when we were still powerless, Christ died for the ungodly. [7] Very rarely will anyone die for a righteous person, though for a good person someone might possibly dare to die. [8] But God demonstrates his own love for us in this: While we were still sinners, Christ died for us.

[9] Since we have now been justified by his blood, how much more shall we be saved from God's wrath through him! [10] For if, while we were God's enemies, we were reconciled to him through the death of his Son, how much more, having been reconciled, shall we be saved through his life! [11] Not only is this so, but we also boast in God through our Lord Jesus Christ, through whom we have now received reconciliation.

What are the first questions that come to mind? What sort of "jumps out" at you and catches your attention?

Capture those initial thoughts and questions here.

GRAPPLING

GOING DEEPER

You can help others in your group go deeper by listening with your full attention and by asking questions as others share. Saying "I wonder about what you just said. Tell me more!" will help people know you care about what they're saying and want them to open up more.

BEHIND THE SCENES

Justification is a judicial term referring to the act of a judge who pardons someone from their offense. It declares that all the claims of the law are satisfied in regards to the justified person. For Paul, God is the judge, who will one day judge all humans according to God's fair, impartial, and holy standards. When people believe in Jesus, they are assured that God's future judgment is declared right now in the present time. The good news is that God's verdict is "not guilty" because of what God himself has already done through the death of Jesus. There is no need to fear the final judgment because we are forgiven here and now by faith in God's merciful and just verdict.

This passage describes humans as "ungodly," "sinners," "powerless," and "God's enemies." Those are pretty strong words. What evidence have you seen to support Paul's claims about the human condition or human nature?

With those thoughts in mind, reread verses 6-8. What new insights do you have on the impact of these verses when you compare them to our condition as humans?

The word "grace" is often defined as God's unmerited favor. How do you think that definition fits what we have just read and discussed?

BEHIND THE SCENES

While in English we only have one word, *love*, to express our emotion for how we feel about those closest to us as well as how we feel about our favorite dessert, the Greeks had several words that expressed the emotion of love. The word used for the way God loves us is *agape*, and it is often thought of as the highest form of love because it denotes an unselfish love for others, one that is generous and helpful to those in need. Has there ever been a greater demonstration of this love than what God did by sending Jesus?

INTERESTING THOUGHTS SPARKED BY OTHERS IN MY GROUP:

BEHIND THE SCENES

Did you notice this passage doesn't say Christ died for the righteous, holy, and clean, but for the opposite? He died for those who are impious, wicked, disrespectful, and irreverent. He died for those who should have been unattractive and repulsive to him, but instead he saw through their sin and loved them with tenderness, mercy, and grace.

How does this change the way you see others who might seem too "dirty" or sinful to come to Jesus?

BEHIND THE SCENES

The word *reconciliation* implies a previous relationship that has been broken. A husband and wife can reconcile a marriage that has been violated. Two friends can reconcile a friendship that has been damaged. But strangers have nothing to reconcile. You might say, "I didn't have a relationship with God before...," but our spirits were made for relationship with him. It's only because of sin that we experienced separation from friendship with God. Through reconciliation we now have a renewed relationship with God, Jesus, the Holy Spirit, and other believers.

GROWING

Have you experienced God's justifying and gracious love? If so, write a few words of thanks to God for accepting and loving you "just as you are."

Write those words of thanks here.

If you have not experienced God's love in the way we discussed, how would you like to respond?

Record your thoughts here.

God loved us when we were his enemies and ultimately commanded us to do the same. Luke 6:27 says, "Love your enemies, do good to those who hate you." Who is someone you need to show love to—not because they deserve it, but possibly because they don't?

Capture your thoughts here.

LESSON 12: IS IT OKAY FOR CHRISTIANS TO SMOKE?

GREETING

What do you consider to be the essential ingredients that absolutely *must* be present in order for a pizza to be called a pizza?

ESSENTIAL MORAL RULES FOR CHRISTIANS	NONESSENTIAL MORAL RULES FOR CHRISTIANS

How is it possible for two Christians to read the same Bible and end up disagreeing about issues of right and wrong?

GROUNDING

God's Word: Romans 14

[1] Accept the one whose faith is weak, without quarreling over disputable matters. [2] One person's faith allows them to eat anything, but another, whose faith is weak, eats only vegetables. [3] The one who eats everything must not treat with contempt the one who does not, and the one who does not eat everything must not judge the one who does, for God has accepted them. [4] Who are you to judge someone else's servant? To their own master, servants stand or fall. And they will stand, for the Lord is able to make them stand.

[5] One person considers one day more sacred than another; another considers every day alike. Each of them should be fully convinced in their own mind. [6] Whoever regards one day as special does so to the Lord. Whoever eats meat does so to the Lord, for they give thanks to God; and whoever abstains does so to the Lord and gives thanks to God. [7] For none of us lives for ourselves alone, and none of us dies for ourselves alone. [8] If we live, we live for the Lord; and if we die, we die for the Lord. So, whether we live or die, we belong to the Lord. [9] For this very reason, Christ died and returned to life so that he might be the Lord of both the dead and the living.

[10] You, then, why do you judge your brother or sister? Or why do you treat them with contempt? For we will all stand before God's judgment seat. [11] It is written:

"'As surely as I live,' says the Lord,
'every knee will bow before me;
every tongue will acknowledge God.'"

[12] So then, each of us will give an account of ourselves to God.

[13] Therefore let us stop passing judgment on one another. Instead, make up your mind not to put any stumbling block or obstacle in the way of a brother or sister. [14] I am convinced, being fully persuaded in the Lord Jesus, that nothing is unclean in itself. But if anyone regards something as unclean, then for that person it is unclean. [15] If your brother or sister is distressed because of what you eat, you are no longer acting in love. Do not by your eating destroy someone for whom Christ died. [16] Therefore do not let what you know is good be spoken of as evil. [17] For the kingdom of God is not a matter of eating and drinking, but of righteousness, peace and joy in the Holy Spirit, [18] because anyone who serves Christ in this way is pleasing to God and receives human approval.

[19] Let us therefore make every effort to do what leads to peace and to mutual edification. [20] Do not destroy the work of God for the sake of food. All food is clean, but it is wrong for a person to eat anything that causes someone else to stumble. [21] It is better not to eat meat or drink wine or to do anything else that will cause your brother or sister to fall.

[22] So whatever you believe about these things keep between yourself and God. Blessed is the one who does not condemn himself by what he approves. [23] But whoever has doubts is condemned if they eat, because their eating is not from faith; and everything that does not come from faith is sin.

What are the first questions that come to mind? What words or phrases catch your attention?

Write your thoughts and ideas here.

BEHIND THE SCENES

The Roman congregation was unique in that Rome, the capital of the pagan empire, also included a strong Jewish colony. Likewise, the cultural and religious composition of the church was Gentile (with their pagan heritage) and Jewish (with their ceremonial laws and Moses' covenant). This diversity in the church was remarkable, especially when we consider the clashes between the two groups that were famously documented in Acts 15. At the heart of the conflict was whether or not a Gentile convert to Christianity needed to also convert to Judaism. This would entail following Jewish ceremonial laws, including male circumcision, kosher food laws, and restrictions regarding Sabbath observance.

While the Council of Jerusalem (Acts 15) ruled that this was not necessary for Gentile converts, a letter from the apostles couldn't instantly erase ancient cultural biases. While the tone of the letter to the Romans suggests the two groups were co-existing peacefully, tensions still existed below the surface. The Jewish Christians were determined to uphold their old ways, which was a challenge in a city where much of the meat found in the marketplace had previously been sacrificed to idols. They responded to this dilemma by abstaining from meat altogether. However, they went a step further and grumbled about the Gentile Christians. This, of course, led the Gentile Christians to judge their Jewish counterparts for being weak in their faith (a point with which Paul—a Jew—happened to agree). Paul's guidance redirected the Gentile Christians to use their relative strength and freedom to serve their weaker brothers.

GOING DEEPER

You might hear someone, even a friend, talk about a freedom they believe they have in Christ that you are certain isn't a freedom at all. Before expressing your disagreement with them, consider asking them to explain how they came to their conclusion. It's okay to disagree, but our goal isn't to win a debate. It's to help each other grow in love and obedience to God.

GRAPPLING

What emotions began to bubble to the surface when it became apparent that people weren't on the same page? What caused you to feel this way?

What kinds of statements tend to heighten tension during conversations like this?

GOING DEEPER

Here are a few suggestions that help keep our conversations peaceable: 1) Preface your opinions by saying, "I might be wrong, but…" or "At this point in my life, this is how I see things…"; 2) Ask people in your group what they think; and 3) Let the other person know you truly heard them by paraphrasing back what you just heard and then asking, "Do I understand you right?"

BEHIND THE SCENES

It may be natural to assume that a person with a long list of religious rules would be spiritually mature. However, in this case, Paul was of the opposite opinion. The Jewish Christians had the weaker faith because they couldn't embrace all the freedom they truly had in Christ. The book of Romans was an open letter that would have been publically read in Christian gatherings all over the capital. Imagine the surprise of the Jewish Christians who attended worship and discovered that the Apostle Paul was calling them out. So, accommodating the weaker brother isn't a matter of pretending you agree with that person. It's choosing to not allow your disagreement or your Christian freedom to become more important than relational unity.

What extra burdens does Paul place on the spiritually strong? Do you think these demands are fair or not?

How can we know if we are among the "stronger" Christians who are free from certain external rules, and not simply placing our own personal preferences in place of God's will?

INTERESTING THOUGHTS SPARKED BY OTHERS IN
MY GROUP:

**How can focusing on building God's kingdom help us avoid
disputes that ultimately don't matter?**

PARTICIPANT GUIDE

GROWING

Am I using my freedom in Christ in a way that is causing damage to someone else's faith?

Write your thoughts here.

Am I allowing any disagreements with other Christians to distract me from what's really important to my faith?

Capture your thoughts here.

What would it look like for me to exercise my freedom while remembering that God is my Lord and Judge?

Record those ideas here.

LESSON 13: WHY WOULD GOD WANT TO MAKE AN EXAMPLE OF ME?

GREETING

What's something you made, at any point in your life, which you were really proud of?

Our church has been given a billboard to advertise the church. What would you put on it?

Write or draw your ideas here.

PARTICIPANT GUIDE

GROUNDING

Ephesians 2:1-10

[1]As for you, you were dead in your transgressions and sins, [2]in which you used to live when you followed the ways of this world and of the ruler of the kingdom of the air, the spirit who is now at work in those who are disobedient. [3]All of us also lived among them at one time, gratifying the cravings of our flesh and following its desires and thoughts. Like the rest, we were by nature deserving of wrath. [4]But because of his great love for us, God, who is rich in mercy, [5]made us alive with Christ even when we were dead in transgressions—it is by grace you have been saved. [6]And God raised us up with Christ and seated us with him in the heavenly realms in Christ Jesus, [7]in order that in the coming ages he might show the incomparable riches of his grace, expressed in his kindness to us in Christ Jesus. [8]For it is by grace you have been saved, through faith—and this is not from yourselves, it is the gift of God— [9]not by works, so that no one can boast. [10]For we are God's handiwork, created in Christ Jesus to do good works, which God prepared in advance for us to do.

What are the first questions that come to mind about Paul's words to the church in Ephesus? What words or phrases catch your attention?

Write those initial thoughts and questions here.

BEHIND THE SCENES

Ephesus, where Paul sent this letter to the Ephesians, was the capital of the Roman province of Asia, which covered the western half of Asia Minor (modern-day southwestern Turkey). It was easy to access by land and sea, so it was commercially, politically, and religiously important. It was a natural place for Paul to go and encourage the growth of the Christian church, where it could influence and spread throughout the surrounding region.

Before Christianity came to Ephesus, it was the center of worship of Artemis of the Ephesians, a local version of the Greek goddess Artemis. Her temple was built there, and, in fact, worship of Artemis was the basis for an entire industry. The temple employed many priests and priestesses, artisans, and others. It attracted pilgrims who brought offerings, and it served as the main source of wealth in the city. The temple served as a sort of bank, where people stored their money for safekeeping, and a museum where beautiful works of art were kept and maintained. It also served as a place of sanctuary for criminals, who could not be arrested when they were within range of the distance a bow could be shot from the temple's walls.

GRAPPLING

GOING DEEPER

During this lesson, it's possible you may realize you haven't been "made alive in Christ" if you have never acknowledged your condition as "deserving of wrath" and sought God's forgiveness for your sin. If you have questions about this, don't wait any longer. Ask the leader of your class to help you understand what it means to begin a new relationship with God through Jesus Christ.

BEHIND THE SCENES

Not many people these days see a need for God's grace. For many, God offers merely a spiritual enhancement to their lives, a nice help if we need him but not strictly necessary. The Bible disagrees. Paul's description of God's grace is about much more than spiritual enhancement. It gives life to the dead. His phrase "dead in your transgressions and sins" in Ephesians 2:1 refers to the universal human condition that is the result of following our own natural desires and preferences.

Spiritual death is not the only way the Bible describes this condition. The New Testament uses several metaphors to describe it:

Blindness (2 Corinthians 4:3-4)

Slavery to sin (Romans 6:17)

Sickness (Mark 2:17)

Being lost (Luke 15:1-32)

Love for darkness (John 3:19-20)

Living as foreigners and strangers (Ephesians 2:12-20)

Deserving of wrath (Ephesians 2:3)

Under the dominion of darkness (Colossians 1:13)

These metaphors present a sobering—and hopeless—picture of the human condition without Jesus. No wonder the Bible speaks of it in terms of death.

What did Paul mean by saying everyone is "by nature deserving of wrath"? Why do you think he said that?

Look at verses 4-7 and the different ways Paul tries to describe God's gift to those who are dead in their transgressions and sins. What does this tell you about God's character and intentions for us?

What does human life look like when someone is "alive with Christ"?

INTERESTING THOUGHTS SPARKED BY OTHERS IN MY GROUP:

PARTICIPANT GUIDE

Paul says we are God's workmanship created to do good works (verse 10). How might this be the way God wants to show "the incomparable riches of his grace" (verse 7) to others? What might this look like in our lives?

BEHIND THE SCENES

Ephesians 2:4 makes clear the reason God rescues us from our deathly condition and offers us new life in Jesus: "Because of his great love for us." We cannot earn the grace and salvation God gives, and we do not receive it because we deserve it. In fact, verse 5 makes clear that he offered this salvation to us when we were dead and not able to offer God anything in return. Even though we were "by nature deserving of wrath," he does not offer us what we deserve. He offers us extravagant love and abundant life, completely undeserved and unearned.

What's more, verse 10 describes God's vision for Christians as the center of God's new creation. We are works of art (workmanship), a model for the new way of being human. This new way is really an old model, for it conforms to what God always intended us to be like. We are called to be living advertisements for God's original design for humanity in relationship with him and with each other.

GROWING

Think about what God's grace means for your life. If God has a purpose for you to serve as an example of his redemptive work, what does that mean for your life? What does it require of you? What does it mean for the ways you spend your time, how you care for your body, what you feed to your mind? How should it change the way you interact with others or share your story?

Capture your thoughts here.

After spending a few moments in silent prayer, write down at least one thing you'll do to position yourself as the example of God's grace he wants you to be.

Write down that one thing here.

NOTES:

_____

_____

_____

_____

_____

_____

_____

_____

_____

_____

_____

_____

_____

_____

NOTES:

NOTES:

_____

_____

_____

_____

_____

_____

_____

_____

_____

_____

_____

_____

_____